Gaenslen

21st Century
Basic Skills
Library

WHAT DO ANIMALS DO IN FALL?

by Rebecca Felix

Cherry Lake Publishing • Ann Arbor, Michigan

1

Published in the United States of America
by Cherry Lake Publishing
Ann Arbor, Michigan
www.cherrylakepublishing.com

Consultant: Marla Conn, Read-Ability

Photo Credits: Jin Young Lee/Shutterstock Images, Cover, Title; David P.
Lewis/Shutterstock Images, 4, 14; Lijuan Guo/Shutterstock Images, 6;
Dmitry Deshevykh/iStockphoto, 8; Celso Pupo/Shutterstock Images, 10;
Ron Sanford/iStockphoto, 12; Mike Bauer/Shutterstock Images, 16; Dennis
Donohue/Shutterstock Images, 18; Angela Brown/iStockphoto, 20

Library of Congress Cataloging-in-Publication Data
Felix, Rebecca, 1984-
  What do animals do in fall? / Rebecca Felix.
      pages cm. -- (Let's look at fall)
  Audience: 5-7.
  Audience: K to grade 3.
  Includes index.
  ISBN 978-1-61080-907-8 (hardback : alk. paper) -- ISBN 978-1-61080-
932-0 (paperback : alk. paper) -- ISBN 978-1-61080-957-3 (ebook) -- ISBN
978-1-61080-982-5 (hosted ebook)
  1. Animal behavior--Juvenile literature. 2. Autumn--Juvenile literature. I.
Title.

  QL751.5.F45 2013
  591.5--dc23

                                          2012030460

Cherry Lake Publishing would like to acknowledge
the work of The Partnership for 21st Century Skills.
Please visit *www.21stcenturyskills.org* for more information.

Printed in the United States of America
Corporate Graphics Inc.
January 2013
CLFA10

TABLE OF CONTENTS

Fall Begins

Fall begins after summer. Days get colder. Animals **prepare** for winter.

Winter Coats

Deer grow **thick** coats to keep warm.

Arctic fox fur turns white. This helps them hide in snow.

What do squirrels eat?

Food for Winter

Squirrels and chipmunks **store** food for winter.

What did the bear catch?

12

Black bears eat a lot. They build up fat. They live off fat in winter.

Hibernating

Woodchucks prepare to **hibernate**. They fall into a deep winter sleep.

What Do You See?

What color leaves do you see?

Box turtles hibernate, too. They find winter homes in fall.

Migrating

Canada geese **migrate**. They fly where it is warmer.

Caribou migrate to find food.
Snow will fall soon!

Find Out More

BOOK

Rustad, Martha E. H. *Animals in Fall: Preparing for Winter*.
  Minneapolis: Millbrook Press, Lerner Publications, 2011.

WEB SITE

Creature Feature—National Geographic Kids
kids.nationalgeographic.com/kids/animals/creaturefeature
Learn about all kinds of animals.

Glossary

hibernate (HYE-bur-nate) to go into a deep, long sleep
  during winter

migrate (MYE-grate) to move to another place

prepare (prih-PAIR) to get ready

store (STOR) to put something away for later

thick (THIK) wide and packed close together

Home and School Connection

Use this list of words from the book to help your child become a better reader. Word games and writing activities can help beginning readers reinforce literacy skills.

animals	deep	grow	squirrels
arctic	deer	hibernate	store
bears	eat	hide	summer
build	fall	homes	thick
Canada	fat	leaves	turns
caribou	fly	live	turtles
chipmunks	food	migrate	warm
coats	fox	prepare	white
colder	fur	sleep	winter
color	geese	snow	woodchucks

What Do You See?

What Do You See? is a feature paired with select photos in this book. It encourages young readers to interact with visual images in order to build the ability to integrate content in various media formats.

You can help your child further evaluate photos in this book with additional activities. Look at the images in the book without the What Do You See? feature. Ask your child to describe one detail in each image, such as a color, time of day, animal, or setting.

Index

About the Author

Rebecca Felix is an editor and writer. She lives in Minnesota. Deer, geese, and squirrels live in Minnesota, too! Rebecca likes seeing geese fly south in fall.